Teach Your Preschooler To Learn

A Parent's Guide

Preparing Your Toddler for School

Author: Jan Sixt

Jan Sixt's Teach To Learn Press
Avon Lake, OH

Teach Your Preschooler to Learn, A Parent's Guide:
Preparing Your Toddler for School

For further information, contact the publisher: Jan Sixt's Teach To Learn Press, www.jstutor.com.

Library of Congress Control Number: 2012924197

ISBN: 978-0-9849361-2-0

Dedicated to all preschoolers.
You represent learning and discovery in its purest form.

Especially dedicated to Ally, Bryan, and Augie.
You add so much to my life.

What Others Say

I found this book to be a refreshingly quick read with ideas that are easy for any parent to follow. The times have changed since I was in kindergarten, and the expectations have changed a great deal too! In my everyday encounters as a mom, I have noticed a gap between children who attend a curriculum-based childcare setting versus those who do not. This creates quite a challenge for kindergarten teachers. Speaking as a parent, I do not want my child to be a step behind. Your book not only would help close this gap, but also ensure that children who are in daycare have learned the appropriate knowledge base before entering kindergarten. Your takeaways at the end of each chapter act as a simple checklist for busy parents. They provide easy to incorporate ideas to help encourage little minds continue the amazing exploration and knowledge they crave!

—JoAnn Ellwood, Parent, Frederick County, Virginia.

Jan Sixt has provided a truly priceless gift to all parents of young children by writing Teach Your Preschooler to Learn. She has shown us how busy, over-stressed parents can expose and teach our little ones in everyday, real-life scenarios. These lessons will carry our little ones onto a successful path into the world of kindergarten.

—Laura Moss, Parent; former first grade teacher of Cleveland Catholic Diocese, and Avon Lake City Schools; former Program Coordinator for LEAPS, Cleveland, Ohio.

A parent is a child's first teacher and this book provides many excellent examples of things you can do in everyday life to help your young child be ready, eager, and successful with both school and the learning process.

—Paula M. Shadle, MLS; Children's Service Manager, Avon Lake Public Library, Avon Lake, Ohio.

Table of Contents

Acknowledgements

With grateful recognition for their heartening support, their motivating interest, and their savvy expertise, I thank:

My children, Kate and John
My daughter-in-law, Thuy
My son-in-law, Anthony
Debra Rohde (www.rohdemd.com)
Robbie Short (www.robbieshort.com)
Carolynn Cheatham (www.cgctutoring.com)
Shelley Hussey (www.shelleyhussey.com)
Paula M. Shadle, MLS
Debra DiLapo
Laura Moss
JoAnn Ellwood
Deena LaVigne
Janet Benjamins

How to Use This Book

The ages between birth and six are a most exciting period of life. Children change rapidly both physically and cognitively during this developmental stage. Most animal species nurture their young for several months to several years before they reach adulthood. The human animal has the unique opportunity to observe this growth and to enhance its offspring's life for nearly two decades. As parents and caregivers, you are your child's first teachers. Your classroom is your home and neighborhood. Your curriculum is the humble flow of your daily lives together.

Teach Your Preschooler to Learn, A Parent's Guide: Preparing Your Toddler for School explains how busy parents can respond to their child's natural curiosity and readiness to learn. You can prepare your child for school easily through casual discussion, manipulative toys, music, decorations, movies, books, and short trips while doing normal daily errands or while taking a walk together. These teaching opportunities are used to expose your child to concepts, and to invite your child to learn more about a subject now and later.

I am a teacher and a private tutor. I wrote this book to inform parents of some essential physical, social, and cognitive skills that schools recommend for their incoming kindergarteners. I understand that parents are very, very busy. Many of you work, have other children to care for, have a house to clean, and have meals to cook. I was in your shoes not so long ago, juggling work, family responsibilities, and the needs of my own two growing children. Let me show you how to better use the time you have to help your baby, toddler, or preschooler attain the necessary skills which are needed to achieve a positive and successful experience when your child does enter kindergarten.

Once children formally enter school, they experience learning by category. There is spelling class, reading class, math class, social studies class, etc. In fact, my first book, *Teach Your Child to Learn, A Parent's Guide: Simple and Tested Techniques That Work* is organized by subject just as a child's school day. I wrote that book in order to help parents of school-aged children. Each chapter describes techniques, starting with an essential one, to help the student capture a "pivotal" skill which will smooth the road to learning more advanced concepts and subject material. Even though these techniques can help students of any age, the younger a person can adopt these suggestions, the more productive a student that person can become. *Teach Your Child to Learn* is a logical extension of *Teach Your Preschooler to Learn*. These books are my sincere efforts to help you help your child, effectively, efficiently, and lovingly.

Mommy, Daddy, be prepared. . . you also are about to grow in the most wonderful ways!

Chapter One

Skills for Incoming Kindergarteners

Most school districts have a list of recommended skills for children as they enter school. Children function better and assimilate more quickly if they enter kindergarten with several proficiencies. As a parent—and your child's first teacher—you can help prepare your child for his/her first formal academic experience, which will begin your child's track in the educational system for another twelve years.

I have separated these skill recommendations into categories. Wouldn't it be helpful to know what is expected of your five-year old before kindergarten enrollment? If you knew, you could better prepare your toddler.

Schools recommend that incoming kindergarteners will:

Physical Skills
- Independently take care of toilet needs
- Self-dress: tie shoes, button, snap, zip
- Hold and use scissors and pencils correctly
- Work neatly using glue, scissors, pencils, and crayons
- Copy shapes and letters
- Hold a book correctly
- Build with blocks
- Catch and throw a ball
- Stand on one foot, skip, gallop, jump, and hop

Social Skills
- Follow three-step directions
- Complete a ten-minute activity with focus
- Attentively listen for a ten-minute period of time
- Respect and take care of personal belongings and those of others
- Show respect for and follow directions of those in authority
- Be able to take turns

Cognitive Skills
- Recognize own name in print
- Write own name

- Recognize most letters
- Know own birth date, phone number, and address
- Recognize shapes, such as rectangle, square, triangle, and circle
- Identify objects and know their actions (example: scissors cut paper)
- Know colors
- Count to at least 20
- Have been exposed to written numerals 0-10
- Have been exposed to rhymes and opposites
- Recognize directional words, such as in, out, up, and down
- Recognize comparison words, such as big, bigger, biggest, smaller, and larger
- Retell a familiar story

The Take-Away

- Most school districts desire that their incoming kindergarten students have attained certain skill levels
- Call your local school district or visit the school's website to get a list of these desired skills

Techniques to Try

1. Be your child's first teacher
2. Use your home and neighborhood as your classroom
3. Use the humble flow of your daily lives together as your curriculum
4. Prepare your child for school easily through casual discussion during quality times of interaction, such as while reading, playing, feeding, and bathing
5. Respond to your child's natural curiosity and readiness to learn using manipulative toys (see Chapter 10), music, decorations, movies, books, and short trips while doing normal daily errands or while taking a walk together
6. Expose your child to *concepts*, and invite your child to learn more about a subject now and later

Chapter Two

Prepare Your Preschooler for Spelling

Social Skills
- Complete a ten-minute activity with focus
- Attentively listen for a ten-minute period of time
- Show respect for and follow directions of those in authority
- Be able to take turns

Cognitive Skills
- Recognize most letters
- Recognize own name in print

Most preschool children become familiar with the alphabet before they enter kindergarten. Alphabet letters adorn babies' clothing, toys, and books. Letters are often part of babies' room decorations, and of course they're on the refrigerator. Point out the letters on signs, auto license plates, appliances, food packages, on the computer keys, in books, on your child's toys, in fact, point letters out wherever you find them. Match capital letters to their lower case counterparts. Some of these matches will be intuitive for your child, such as Cc, Jj, Kk, Mm, Oo, Pp, Ss, Tt, Uu, Vv, Ww, Xx, Yy, and Zz. The look of some letter-matches is less closely related, such as Ff, Ii, Ll, and Nn. Several of the "letter mates" will need to be learned, such as Aa, Bb, Dd, Ee, Gg, Hh, Qq, and Rr.

If your child isn't interested in learning the alphabet letters, keep trying other ways to present them. Perhaps you could wear letter-sticker matches on your own clothing. See when your child notices the upper and lower case *Mm* or *Ss* on your shirt. Perhaps your child will want to wear a set of letters, too. In fact, you could have a marvelous, magical, magnificent, *Mm* day. You could say good *morning*, drink *milk*, put *maple* syrup on pancakes, eat *macaroni*, *mash* some potatoes, get the *mail*, look at a *manhole* cover, read a *map*, read about a *microscope*, and hug your *mama*. You could wear a different letter combination for 26 days.

As long as you have letter stickers, why not place them on some of your child's possessions to represent the initial sounds. For example, place a *d* on the doll, a *t* on the table, and a *b* on the bed. Expand the activity by placing a *ch* on her chair, a *bl* on the blocks, or a *dr* on the drum. Place stand-up alphabet letters near the table to mark the foods that your child is eating for lunch. Perhaps your child could choose the letters himself to represent the sounds of his foods. (Mealtimes are great opportunities to flip letter flashcards since many toddlers are wearing the seat belts on their booster chairs and are more focused on you.)

Form letters with clay, serve alphabet macaroni, bake letter-shaped cookies, purchase letter bath toys, string an alphabet bead necklace, play with letter apps, place Scrabble tiles on the game board, or watch *Wheel of Fortune*. Keep trying to introduce the letters. One of these ideas will probably interest your child. If it's not the first or second technique that interests him, simply pivot to the next idea.

Recognizing the letters and naming them are the initial steps in preparing your child for spelling. The next steps occur when your child knows the sounds that these letters make. When your child can apply the rules for phonics, he will be able to use this valuable tool for decoding, pronouncing, reading, and spelling words. Using phonics is an essential skill. Let me show you how to accomplish introducing this concept to your child.

Children hear the alphabet song and many sing it with zeal, until they get to that *l-m-n-o-p* part. For many, that section of the song is a jumble of incoherent sounds which distort the sounds of the individual letters. Also, some children have difficulty distinguishing the sounds of *b* and *d* or hearing the difference between the short vowel sound of *a* in c*a*t and the short vowel sound of *e* in b*e*d.

First, I want to share what I have found to be the most useful elements of phonics. We'll look at the basic tools of phonics and how to use them; then we'll get to the exceptions.

Consonants

b box	**j** jump	**r** rabbit
c cat (hard "k" sound)	**k** kite	**s** sun
city (soft "s" sound)	**l** little	**t** turtle
d dot	**m** man	**v** van
f five	**n** nut	**w** water
g goat (hard "g" sound)	**p** pie	**x** x-ray
giraffe (soft "j" sound)	**q** queen ("kwee" sound)	**y** yellow
h happy	quiche ("kee" sound)	**z** zipper

14

Blends (Letter combinations that make a blended sound)

bl black	**pr** present	**spl** splash
br brown	**qu** quite	**spr** spring
ch cheese	**sc** scary	**squ** square
cl clock	**sk** ski	**st** stop
cr cry	**scr** scribble	**str** straw
dr draw	**sh** shut	**sw** sweater
fl fly	**shr** shrimp	**th** they
fr frog	**sl** sled	**thr** throw
gl glue	**sm** small	**tr** train
gr green	**sn** snow	**tw** twig
pl play	**sp** spider	**wh** white

Silent Letter Blends

gn gnat *("g" is silent../nat)*   **wr wr**ap *("w" is silent../rap)*
kn knot *("k" is silent../not)*   **ps Ps**alm *("p" is silent../salm)*

Vowels (*a, e, i, o, u,* and sometimes *y*)
Short Vowels

a cat	**o** hot
e men	**u** nut
i pig	

Long Vowels

a cake	**o** open
e street	**u** cube
i ice	

"R" Controlled Vowels

"ar" car	**"ir"** girl
"or" horn	**"ur"** church
"er" locker	

Sometimes "y"

y   my, by *(sound of long i)*   **y; y** mystery *(short i and long e)*
y   busy *(sound of long e)*   **y; y** mystify *(short i and long i)*

Short vowel sounds are usually in words having only one vowel, such as these: *bat, egg, sit, pot,* and *stump.*

They also often occur in words with only one vowel per syllable. For example,

the two syllables in *seven* (sev-en), *singing* (sing-ing), and *jacket* (jack-et) all contain short vowels in both syllables.

Long vowel sounds usually occur in words having two vowels per word or per syllable. For example, the words *bake, goat, and maintain* (main-tain) have long vowel sounds.

A long vowel sound can be spelled with two vowels next to each other, such as in the word *goat*, or with a vowel-consonant-*e*, such as in the word *bake*. In both cases, the first vowel is sounded, but the second vowel . . . the *a* in *goat* or the final *e* in *bake* . . . make no sound at all. In other words, the second vowels remain "silent."

The **"R"** controlled vowels commonly appear in many English words. The sounds of the vowels *(ar, er, ir, or, ur)* are distinctive when the vowel is followed by an *r*. Interestingly, the *er* (m**er**chant), *ir* (sh**ir**t), and *ur* (t**ur**n) all make the same sound. The *ar* (b**ar**n) and *or* (c**or**n) each make their own individual sound.

Sometimes the letter *y* is used as a vowel. It typically mimics the long *e* (dizz**y**), long *i* (st**y**le), or short *i* (m**y**stic).

Oddballs (Common—but weird!—vowel combinations)

au	Paul, au**t**o
ew	new, flew

oo	look, book	(Both pairs of words are spelled with *oo*, but
oo	cool, stool	they make different sounds.)

oi	oil, soil	(Both pairs of words are spelled differently, but
oy	toy, boy	the *oi* and *oy* sound the same.)

ou	ouch, cloud	(Both pairs of words are spelled differently, but
ow	cow, flower	the *ou* and *ow* sound the same.)

ow	snow, flow	(Has long *o* sound.)

These vowel combinations are very strange, but occur in many of the "sight" words in books for the novice reader. Your toddler will encounter these words in normal speech (see Reading Chapter 5), and they are part of the unusual sound combinations that your preschooler will eventually have to recognize and pronounce. When your child understands the information above, he will be well prepared for a typical elementary school spelling list test.

In addition to learning the sounds of the consonants, blends, and vowels, some children may completely misunderstand some word phrases. One of my private tutoring students asked me how to spell *onceuponatime*. He was surprised to learn that the four separate smaller words *once upon a time* comprised the phrase. When you speak, do you slur the sounds? Do you say *e*nvite, when you really mean *i*nvite? Does your child hear *liberry* when you really mean *library*? I've received many email forwards—and so have you—which display the humorous misunderstandings that children have with the words in the *Lord's Prayer*, the *Pledge of Allegiance*, or in an overheard adult conversation.

Parents can painlessly help their toddler prepare for spelling by speaking clearly. Normal conversation will give your child the opportunity to hear the sounds spoken correctly. Your preschooler will mimic the sounds. Make an effort to pronounce the letter sounds correctly. Speak slowly and let your child see how the sounds are formed with your lips and tongue. Some phonetic sounds are more difficult for a child to reproduce, and she may need lots of practice until she can control her mouth and tongue. Among the more difficult sounds to form are *l, r, s, v, y, bl, ch, sh*, and *th*. For example, the sound of *r* is often confused with that of *w*. Raccoon becomes *waccoon*. Furthermore, the sound of the blend *bl*, as in the words *blue* or *blank*, is formed when the tongue hits the roof of the mouth while the lips press together. In another example, the sound of the *th* in the word *think* or *thimble*, may take some explanation. I have told many children that they have to "stick the tip of their tongue out, and blow over it" to make this sound. Then I demonstrate. (It's not my most feminine look, but it usually gets the job done!)

The Take-Away
- Introduce learning the alphabet letters naturally within the course of the day's normal activities
- Speak clearly
- Speak slowly
- Explain and demonstrate the position of the tongue, teeth, and lips
- Encourage your child to model your speech and to practice making the sounds correctly
- Incorporate this parent "modeling" during the daily quality times of interaction, such as while reading, playing, feeding, and bathing
- Your child will be more focused during these times . . . a plus for the busy parent!

Techniques to Try

Point out the letters:
1. On signs
2. On auto license plates
3. On appliances
4. On food packages
5. On the computer keys
6. On your child's toys
7. In books
8. Wherever you find them

Match capital letters to their lower case counterparts:

9. Intuitive matches: Cc, Jj, Kk, Mm, Oo, Pp, Ss, Tt, Uu, Vv, Ww, Xx, Yy, Zz
10. Less closely related matches: Ff, Ii, Ll, Nn
11. "Letter-mates" that need to be learned: Aa, Bb, Dd, Ee, Gg, Hh, Qq, Rr
12. Wear letter-sticker matches on your own clothing: Mm

Other ideas:

13. Have a marvelous, magical, magnificent, *Mm* day. You could say good *morning*, drink *milk*, put *maple* syrup on pancakes, eat *macaroni, mash* some potatoes, get the *mail*, look at a *manhole* cover, read a *map*, read about a *microscope*, and hug your *mama*
14. Wear a different letter combination for 26 days
15. Place a *d* on the doll, a *t* on the table, and a *b* on the bed
16. Expand the activity by placing a *ch* on her chair, a *bl* on the blocks, or a *dr* on the drum
17. Place stand-up alphabet letters near the table to mark the foods that your child is eating for lunch
18. Let your child choose the letters himself to represent the sounds of his foods
19. Form letters with clay
20. Serve alphabet macaroni
21. Bake letter-shaped cookies
22. Purchase letter bath toys
23. String an alphabet bead necklace
24. Play with letter apps
25. Place Scrabble tiles on the game board
26. Watch *Wheel of Fortune*
27. Keep trying to introduce the letters

Chapter Three

Prepare Your Preschooler for Writing

Physical Skills
- Self-dress: tie shoes, button, snap, zip
- Hold and use scissors and pencils correctly
- Catch and throw a ball

Social Skills
- Respect and take care of personal belongings and those of others

Cognitive Skills
- Many of the skills in this chapter exceed those recommended by most school districts

Very young babies do not have much control over their muscular movements. Their kicks, flailing arms, and torso movements appear random and without much purpose. In reality, these actions are strengthening their gross motor muscles. Within the first six months of life, a baby will gain much control over these gross motor skills and will continue to perfect them as he grows. The fine motor skills that allow a toddler to purposely pick up a small object, like a button or a piece of finger food, use the smaller muscles of the hands and fingers. These muscles develop after the large muscles of the body. As your child grows, you should be encouraging him to practice using these small motor muscles because these will be used when your child holds a pair of scissors, a crayon, or a pencil.

If your child is interested in writing letters or numbers, encourage him to use the proper pencil grip. The way in which your child manipulates pencils, markers, and crayons changes as his small motor muscles mature. This is normal. If you are interested in this topic, I encourage you to do some independent research. The Internet can help you locate websites that show detailed pictures of the proper grips for the developing child.

Prewriting exercises can be found in many preschool curriculum-based workbooks. They usually show a series of traceable vertical, horizontal, diagonal, and curved lines. Then many workbooks will introduce traceable letters and numbers. Encourage your child to follow the directional arrows when he copies these symbols. Your child may also enjoy practicing his writing using washable markers on a wipe-off board.

The purpose of this chapter is to prepare your child for the writing experience both physically and cognitively. Although much information is available regarding gross and small motor muscle development, there is another important consideration for parents which will help prepare their child for writing. The use of proper grammar can really impact your child's future education. As soon as your child understands a several-word phrase like, "Bobby bath" or "Anna new shoes," begin speaking to your child in complete sentences.

> Say: "It is time for Bobby to take a bath," or "It's time for Bobby's bath."
> Say: "Anna has new shoes," or "Anna's new shoes are pretty."

It is also time to forego the baby talk now. There is a use for baby talk from a child who has little receptive language skills. However, if this is the time that you judge is a "turning point" and that your child is ready for proper grammar, make sure that your child knows it. There is a distinction between when you need to use baby talk and when—cute as it may be—it becomes a hindrance to your child's learning.

Pay attention to your own use of grammar. Your child will mimic your speech patterns. For example, *well* is an adverb so it describes an action. ("She dances well.") The word *good* is an adjective so it describes a noun (person, place, thing, quality, or idea). ("She is a good dancer.") Furthermore, children often misuse pronouns saying "Me like you" when they should be saying, "I like you." (*I, she, he, it, we,* and *they* are subjective pronouns and are used as the subject of a sentence.) The subject of the sentence usually comes before the verb, or action, of the sentence. Let's say that the word *run* is the action of the sentence. Encourage your toddler to say ***I** run,* **we** *run,* **they** *run,* **she/he/it** *runs*. What if you said, "The dog runs to me/him/her/us/them"? (*Me, him, her, us,* and *them* are objective pronouns.) Therefore, those pronouns are not used before the verb of the sentence. The words *you* and *it* are exceptions to this basic rule because both words can be used as a subject and as an object in a sentence. For example, "***You** run to Bob" and "Bob runs to **you**." "**It** is chocolate ice cream" and "I like the taste of **it**." (In my first book *Teach Your Child to Learn, A Parent's Guide: Simple and Tested Techniques That Work*, I explain other practical applications of grammar that advances this topic for school-aged children.)

Subjective Pronouns	**Objective Pronouns**
I	me
you	you
he/she/it	him/her/it
we	us
they	them

Another example of poor grammar is the popular expression, "Do you want this, or **no**?" This thought is better expressed by saying, "Do you want this, or not?" If you are not sure about the correct grammar, it is easy to check yourself by searching the Internet.

Sometimes a child will apply the rules of grammar and spelling for a "regular" verb to that of an "irregular" verb. Normally, to form a regular, past tense verb, simply add *ed* to the end of the verb. For example, *play* becomes *played*. ("She *played* at the park all afternoon.") However, the verb *drink*, does not become *drinked*. It is incorrect to say, "She *drinked* all of her milk." This verb is irregular and is properly used in the following example: "She *drank* all of her milk." If your child makes this error, simply explain that the grammar is different in this situation, or better yet, immediately use the correct form in conversation with your child. In this way you will not be obviously correcting your child, but she will hear the correct usage of the word in context. You will probably be surprised how quickly and smoothly your child incorporates the correct usage into her speech.

Other Irregular Verbs

Present Tense	**Past Tense**
be	was, were
become	became
begin	began
bite	bit
break	broke
bring	brought
build	built
buy	bought
catch	caught
choose	chose
come	came
cost	cost

cut	cut
dig	dug
do	did
draw	drew
drive	drove
eat	ate
fall	fell
feed	fed
feel	felt
fight	fought
find	found
forget	forgot
forgive	forgave
freeze	froze
get	got
give	gave
go	went
grow	grew
hang	hung
hear	heard
hide	hid
hit	hit
hold	held
hurt	hurt
keep	kept
know	knew
lead	led
leave	left
let	let
lose	lost
make	made
meet	met
pay	paid
put	put
quit	quit
read	read
ride	rode
ring	rang

rise	rose
run	ran
say	said
see	saw
sell	sold
send	sent
shake	shook
sing	sang
sit	sat
sleep	slept
slide	slid
speak	spoke
spend	spent
stand	stood
strike	struck
sweep	swept
swim	swam
take	took
teach	taught
tear	tore
tell	told
think	thought
throw	threw
understand	understood
wake	woke
wear	wore
win	won
write	wrote

Lastly, some children confuse, or make up words which they are having trouble saying. I've heard a child say "smashmellows" when she meant *marshmallows*, "spagggi" when she meant *spaghetti* and "hoptocopter" when he meant *helicopter*. After you have had a good laugh—and you also have had your fill of hearing your child's wonderful interpretations—you again must incorporate the correct pronunciation into your conversation. Hearing these mangled words is one of the blessings of childhood that parents truly enjoy, so it may take a while before you are willing to correct this one. (I <u>totally</u> understand!)

The Take-Away
- Give tasks which help your child develop small motor muscles
- Speak in full sentences
- Use proper grammar
- Correct your child subtly by immediately incorporating the proper grammar into your conversation with your child

Techniques to Try

To exercise the large motor muscles:
1. Visit the playground
2. Toss a ball back and forth
3. Allow your toddler to lift and carry her possessions
4. Expect your child to clean up his toys before bedtime

To exercise the small motor muscles:
5. Allow your toddler to purposely pick up small objects, like a button or a piece of finger food
6. String beads
7. Cut with a pair of scissors
8. Use crayons or pencils correctly
9. Button, snap, and zip clothing
10. Dress independently
11. Tie shoes
12. Play with puzzles that have knobs for hand grasps
13. Eat with a spoon and a fork

Grammar:
14. Speak to your child in complete sentences
15. Emphasize using subjective and objective pronouns correctly
16. Emphasize using irregular verbs correctly
17. Correct your child's mispronunciations by using the words correctly in your speech with your child

Chapter Four

Prepare Your Preschooler for Thinking

Social Skills
- Follow three-step directions
- Complete a ten-minute activity with focus
- Attentively listen for a ten-minute period of time

Cognitive Skills
- Recognize own name in print
- Recognize most letters
- Know own birthdate, phone number, and address
- Recognize shapes, such as rectangle, square, triangle, and circle
- Identify objects and know their actions
- Know colors
- Recognize directional words, such as in, out, up, and down
- Recognize comparison words, such as big, bigger, biggest, smaller, and larger
- Retell a familiar story

It must be very confusing to be a baby who has little understanding about the surroundings that he now occupies. Furthermore, in an instant the rules changed too. *You mean I have to wear clothes? How did you say I have to eat now? At least this pooping and peeing thing hasn't changed much . . . for now! What are those new sounds and smells? I'm too hot. I'm too cold. Who the heck are those big, moving things handling me anyway? Everything looks rather blurry. I feel like a paperweight!*

Information gathered from the five senses of taste, touch, sight, hearing, and smell, form sensory memory. It is the first step in the complicated process of remembering. Sensory memory holds very few items at a time and these memories fade within seconds. (Is it any surprise that parents need to *show* and *tell* their children the same things over and over again?)

If a person is paying attention, the information gathered from the five senses is transferred to one's short-term memory. If a person continues to actively think about the collected information, it will remain in short-term memory. However, the information fades in approximately twenty seconds if one is distracted. Information is held in terms of sound, or acoustically, in the short-term memory. (Is this why we can hear ourselves think?) As in sensory memory, short-term memory holds few meaningful "chunks" of information at a time. Short-term memory is *active* memory and is called "working memory" by some. The information held in active, short-term memory is similar to the number of open files on a computer monitor at any given time. Its information can be actively manipulated, especially if this information is organized into meaningful categories. In my book, *Teach Your Child to Learn, A Parent's Guide: Simple and Tested Techniques That Work*, I suggest that these categories include:

- *Facts*: Mittens is the cat's name
- *Reasons*: It is raining so water is falling out of the sky
- *Conditional Ideas*: If I throw my cup of milk, Mommy will not replace it
- *Cause and Effect*: I did throw my cup of milk; Mommy did not replace it
- *Categories*: Fruit—banana, apple, grapes; Clothing items—pants, socks, shirt, belt
- *Associations*: Stop at red traffic lights
- *Symbols*: Y, 3, $, =, +
- *Abbreviations*: Mr., Rev., USA
- *Short Phrases/Groupings*: States of the union, first cousins, 30 different flavors
- *Relationships*:

Opposites:	up/down; sweet/sour
Size:	small, medium, large
Family:	grandmother/mother/daughter; brother/sister
Use:	stove is for cooking; wrench loosens or tightens pipe
Age:	old/new; old/young
Part of a Whole:	leg is part of table
Whole to Part:	loaf of bread has many slices
Function:	acorn grows oak tree
Kinds:	eagles and ducks are kinds of birds
Symbols:	good luck/four-leaf clover; bad luck/number 13
Real to Fantasy:	horse/unicorn
How:	car travels on a road; train travels on a track
Synonyms:	envy/jealousy; nice/pleasant
Time:	second, minute, hour; day, month, year
Degree:	warm, hot, scalding; good, better, best
Sequence:	elementary, secondary, college; first, second, third
Characteristic:	porcupine has quills
Purpose:	seat belt for protection

Long-term memory, in contrast to sensory and short-term memory, has a nearly unlimited capacity for holding information. If this information is deeply processed by the individual, it is more likely to become part of long-term memory. For example, if you cover a toy as your baby reaches for it and let her "find" it, you will be encouraging your baby to problem solve. Perhaps you could put a pull-toy under the couch, leaving the string exposed, and let your baby pull the string until she gets the toy. Your toddler will practice thinking when she matches patterns with geometric blocks or makes original patterns with beads or colored chips. Sorting pictures, using nesting cups, building with blocks or boxes, drawing pictures, counting to ten, washing her hands, and dressing herself are a few more examples of problem solving activities that add practical experiences for building long-term memories.

Learning can facilitate a permanent change in behavior or knowledge. As your baby grows, she may experience classical conditioning, operant conditioning, and observational learning. Via her five senses of taste, touch, sight, hearing, and smell, your child will gather stimuli which will serve as her initial information for learning, memory, and thinking. (This is why it is so important for a parent to rule out a physical impairment—perhaps to hearing or sight—before optimum learning can begin.)

In classical conditioning your child uses these "gathered" stimuli to predict a relationship between the stimuli and an event. For example, she may emotionally connect the sound that the neighbor's yard wind chimes make on a windy day with the scary, startling slam of her bedroom door. In the future, when the wind chimes sound, your child becomes frightened. Similarly, in his famous experiment, the scientist Pavlov conditioned a dog to salivate at the sound of a bell.

In operant conditioning your child responds because the event is reinforced. For example, a lab animal learns that it will get food when it steps on a lever. Behavior modification techniques and computer-assisted instruction have used operant conditioning successfully with children. Perhaps your child could receive a sticker to place on a chart when he successfully makes his pee-pee in the toilet, or you clap when he puts on his socks by himself. Reinforcement can have either positive or negative consequences. Some psychologists believe that giving positive rewards to the learner is more effective than punishing unwanted responses. However, both types of reinforcements can affect the learner's behavior and facilitate change. Perhaps you have longed to have more peaceful interactions with your child at bedtime. Sometimes simply keeping the environment clear of distractions is the key. For example, the television could be turned off and soothing background music could be enjoyed during the bedtime routines. Then a story could be read. When parents are searching for the correct combination of reinforcements to use with their child, the parents need to assess their techniques to be sure that their methods of re-inforcements are getting results while minimizing any negative side effects.

Observational learning, sometimes called modeling or social learning, takes place when your child imitates the behavior of others. Many of your child's daily actions—perhaps properly holding eating utensils or washing hands—are learned through observation. The effect of watching violence on television is an example of a controversial issue regarding observational learning.

When developing the ability to think independently, a toddler needs to practice solving problems. You should encourage your toddler to lengthen her attention span. When she is involved in an activity, try not to interrupt her thought process. Give her the freedom to fumble and experience failure. Allow your preschooler to explore her environment to the extent which time and safety permits.

As a rule, younger children need more help and supervision because they have more physical and emotional needs. However, babies, toddlers, and school-aged children change very rapidly. Parents should educate themselves about child development so they can limit the amount of help they give their child as she grows and becomes more capable. It is beneficial to the child to explore her own environment. For example, parents should let their baby crawl for the toy instead of outright handing it to her. It is important not to anticipate the baby's every wish. Her lack of ability to communicate may frustrate her, but that will encourage the child to speak.

Providing the right amount of assistance to your child as she continues to develop her own problem-solving skills is a balancing act. The main point is to be aware that your child is making developmental strides that allow her to physically and mentally handle more responsibility. She will best learn to solve problems if she is permitted to do so. Using your parental judgment will allow her to try, perhaps fail, finally succeed, and to benefit from the total experience.

"Success breeds success" is one of my personal philosophies. I've learned that when a child tastes success, she is willing to try another skill that may seem to be just out of reach. Parenting involves meeting the physical and emotional needs of your child, without stifling the child's growth towards independence. When a child struggles and succeeds, her attention span will lengthen, preparing her for the challenges of formally entering school.

Reasoning allows a student to find order, comprehend the truth about past events, understand cause and effect in the present, and prepare for future events. Reasoning fosters an ability to analyze, critique, draw inferences, clarify, prioritize, connect ideas, and recognize motive. Questioning develops a higher level of thinking, and is an important lifetime skill.

So how does your child learn to use logical reasoning?

Some activities use prediction. Ask your toddler what to expect when the doorbell rings, or when the neighbors put out their garbage cans. Use wordless books to encourage your child to make up his own narrative. Talk about what you see or what is likely to be happening in the story. Here are a few examples of wordless picture books:

1. Mayer   *A Boy, A Dog and A Frog* (series)
2. dePaloa   *Pancakes for Breakfast*
3. Sis   *Beach Ball*
4. Mayer   *The Great Cat Chase*
5. Goodall   *Naughty Nancy*
6. Kent   *The Scribble Monster*
7. Winter   *The Bear and the Fly*
8. Krahn   *A Flying Saucer Full of Spaghetti*

Sequential ordering can continue the process. For example, ask your child to talk, step by step, about family routines. Discuss the day's activities: rising, dressing, eating, working, school, sleeping, etc. Later a child could describe the steps in baking cookies, playing on a slide, or using an umbrella. Sequential ordering of sets of pictures is fun for children. An older child may be required in class to list the steps used to solve an involved story problem—a useful task in logic and reasoning.

Orienting puzzle pieces until they fit correctly, holding a book so the pages are viewed right-side up, turning the pages of a books from right to left, building with blocks, rolling a ball, and manipulating the environment all help a child develop logical reasoning.

Sleep aids the thinking process, too. If adults sleep the recommended 8 hours per night, we will spend one-third of our lives sleeping. While asleep, the body is less active and less responsive to the surroundings, but the brain is not passive. Neuron activity in the brain can be quite strong.

Regular cycles, called circadian rhythms, repeat themselves regularly, usually every 24 hours. These circadian rhythms are influenced by the duration of light of the day, the darkness of the night, clocks, mealtimes, and other external reinforcements of time. However, circadian rhythms can be disrupted by factors like jet lag or shift schedules. These interruptions place stresses on the body as workers or travelers try to sleep during the daytime while most others are awake. (I'm sure all of you sleep deprived new parents have a lot of sympathy for those sleep deprived travelers right now!)

There are differences in individual sleep requirements. Newborn babies sleep 15 hours a day, while the elderly average about 6 hours. According to the Mayo Clinic (www.mayoclinic.com), toddlers need 12 to 14 hours of sleep daily and school-age children require 10 to 11 hours per day. There are also differences regarding when individuals sleep. Some people function best during the morning hours; others work well later at night.

Sleep, over the course of a normal night, consists of five stages in which a person experiences different types of brain activity. Eye movements, tension of the muscles, and the electrical activity of brain waves can be measured by electroencephalography (EEG) in sleep laboratories. As a person falls asleep (Stage 1), brain waves become irregular and the person could wake easily. In Stage 2, the brain waves can be recorded in rapid bursts. Delta waves and complete muscle relaxation occurs in Stage 3 sleep. Stage 4 is known as deep sleep in which the EEG shows mostly delta waves. During this period someone is very difficult to awaken. Typically, a person experiences Stage 1 through Stage 4 before reversing the steps back toward the small, irregular brain waves of Stage 1. At this time a person enters Stage 5, or Rapid Eye Movement (REM) sleep. Under the eyelids, the eyes move back and forth rapidly.

When sleep deprivation occurs, in as little as two days the performance on tasks quickly declines unless the task is highly interesting. Sleep restores the body, bringing a person physically back to normal after exertion, and enables awareness and concentration for mental activities. Loss of sleep negatively effects the ability of children to learn and can interfere with their daily activities. As a parent, you can empower your child when you set predictable schedules for sleep.

The Take-Away
- Stimulate your child's five senses
- Encourage your child to categorize information into useful memories through logical reasoning
- Help your child lengthen his attention span
- Reduce the amount of assistance that you offer as your child becomes more capable
- Encourage independence and self-reliance
- Insist that your child get the proper amount of sleep

Techniques to Try

1. Use different words when talking to your child; let him hear variety in your vocabulary
2. Leave the string of a pull-toy exposed, and let your baby pull the string until she gets the toy
3. Let your baby crawl for his toy instead of outright handing it to him
4. Pretend you do not understand so your baby will speak in words
5. Match patterns with geometric blocks
6. Make original patterns with beads or colored chips
7. Sort pictures
8. Use nesting cups
9. Build with blocks or boxes
10. Draw pictures
11. Count to ten
12. Let your child wash her hands
13. Let your child dress herself
14. Ask your toddler what to expect when the doorbell rings or when the neighbors put out their garbage cans
15. Use wordless books to encourage your child to make up her own narrative
    a. Talk about what she sees or what is likely to be happening in the story
    b. Talk about what she thinks the characters are thinking or feeling
    c. Ask her what clues the pictures are giving her to support her statements
16. Ask your child to talk, step by step, about family routines
17. Discuss the day's activities: rising, dressing, eating, working, school, sleeping, etc
18. Describe the steps in baking cookies
19. Describe the steps when playing on a slide
20. Explain how to use an umbrella
21. Orient puzzle pieces until they fit correctly
22. Hold a book so the pages are viewed right-side up
23. Turn the pages of a book from right to left
24. Roll a ball
25. Let your child turn the wall light switch off as you leave the room
26. Let your child view himself in a mirror
27. To the best of your circumstances, adhere to your child's sleep needs
28. Prepare your child for sleep with a comforting routine, perhaps a bath and/or story
29. Help your child relax so she can learn how to fall asleep

Chapter Five

Prepare Your Preschooler for Reading

Physical Skills
- Hold a book correctly

Social Skills
- Complete a ten-minute activity with focus
- Attentively listen for a ten-minute period of time
- Respect and take care of personal belongings and those of others
- Show respect for and follow directions of those in authority
- Be able to take turns

Cognitive Skills
- Recognize own name in print
- Recognize most letters
- Recognize shapes, such as rectangle, square, triangle, and circle
- Identify objects and know their actions
- Know colors
- Count to at least 20
- Have been exposed to written numerals 0-10
- Have been exposed to rhymes and opposites
- Recognize directional words, such as in, out, up, and down
- Recognize comparison words, such as big, bigger, biggest, smaller, and larger
- Retell a familiar story

Let's review. Toddlers learn to reproduce speech sounds when they watch and hear others clearly pronounce their words. Young children also mimic the grammar of those they hear. Additionally, practical experiences of life build long-term memories. Okay. . . Got it! But at one or two years old, how many *practical life experiences* could a child have when his large and small motor muscles are still not completely mature?

Books can easily bridge this gap. At first, books will give your child a recognizable bank of "picture" words. Babies may learn to point to the cat, ball, or shoe in their own homes, but books can expand the child's vocabulary to include shawl, conveyor belt, glacier, or other items that you may not even want in your house! (Much of a child's formal education involves recognizing, understanding, and using the vocabulary from the different disciplines. Terms like Bunsen burner, continent, and circulatory system are terms just like cat, ball, and shoe are terms. When in school the older child, like the toddler, will need to recognize and incorporate the term's meaning into his working vocabulary before the concepts can be understood.)

Nonfiction, informational books can expose your child to forest animals, the oceans, careers of people in the community, the solar system, the organs inside of his own body, and many, many other fascinating topics. Fictional stories can introduce your child to other children, animals, or creatures. Your child will be allowed to tag along as these characters have adventures, meet challenges, work through their problems, sometimes succeed, and perhaps fail. Even though these experiences are not your child's actual adventures, your child will benefit from experiencing them through the story's message. Through the magic of reading, your child may watch his "fictional peer" understand how to use the potty, dress himself, throw a ball, and learn to jump. The story may involve the storybook child's struggle with respecting his property or the belongings of others. The stories may deal with controlling anger, taking turns, accepting a new sibling, or explaining when it is time to be quiet. The combinations are endless, but the point is that reading books to your child can expand his world view when his physical mobility is limited.

The **elements of the story** are basic to full understanding and appreciation of the narrative.

> PLOT—significant action
> CHARACTER—people, animals
> SETTING—time and place where story occurs
> THEME—controlling idea or central insight
> POINT OF VIEW—who actually tells the story

All of these elements intertwine, but each deserves individual attention. (See *Teach Your Child to Learn, A Parent's Guide: Simple and Tested Techniques That Work* for a more in-depth discussion of the story elements as it applies to school-aged children.)

For the preschool level listener or beginning reader, use the following list when discussing the story. You will get a good idea of how well your child understood what you just read to her, or more importantly, what she just read to you!

Who: Who was in the story?
Where: Where was that character?
What: What was that person's (animal's) problem? What did that person (animal) do?
When: When did that happen?
Why: Why did that happen?
How: How did that happen?

The discussions that these questions will generate can be a time of great mental growth for your child. You will become aware of your child's perceptions, be able to clarify misunderstandings, expand concepts, tackle your child's problem areas without directly critizing your child, as well as help your child learn about the complex categories regarding the organization of thought (see Chapter 4).

Literally from birth, reading to baby gives the exhausted parents an opportunity to speak to their baby without having to think about what to say. The tones and cadence of the human voice are stimulating to the baby. Furthermore, Mom and Dad will be able to read what they want to read and the baby will not know the difference. As the baby grows, he will enjoy snuggling with his parents as the colorful pages of a book entertain him. The baby is now hearing some of the words from his actual experiences and steadily connecting the "mental" dots to understand that the words can be associated with the pictures. Now the parents can point out the details within the pictures—doggy's eyes, Shelley's eyes; doggy's paw, Shelley's foot. The beginnings of *reasoning* involving the *relationship* and the *category* have begun!

Reading books to your preschooler gives you an opportunity to speak the language clearly, pronouncing the consonants and vowel sounds (see Chapter 2) so your child can practice hearing them. Normally the grammar (see Chapter 3) has been screened and is correct in most books. If you are reading a book in which the grammar is purposely incorrect, as in the *Junie B. Jones* series by Barbara Park, you can use this as a teaching opportunity to laugh and correct Junie B. instead of your child.

Many books for very young children incorporate directional and comparison words, as well as rhymes and opposites. This exposes your child to several other skills which schools prefer that their incoming kindergarteners know. Picture books often introduce other cognitive skills including alphabet, number, and shape recognition. Select some books that use pronouns (see Chapter 3) and are written in complete sentences in order to expose your preschooler to this language developmental step.

Toddlers Begin to Read

If you stress the consonant, letter blends, and vowel sounds in your speech, you may notice that your preschooler will begin to recognize these combinations on the printed page. This is an early step in the reading process. Your young child is showing a natural curiosity and readiness to learn to read. It is very exciting to watch a child develop another level of independence. The ability to read opens a child's world exponentially.

Parents can help their child succeed when they gather books that use vocabulary which supports the consonant, letter blends and vowel sounds the child has been practicing. Many libraries and bookstores have a designated "children's section" where books are sorted and color coded according to the difficulty of their reading content. For example, books may be categorized as *early readers, beginning readers, advanced readers, etc.* This helps busy parents select the appropriate reading level and smoothly advance their child when she has mastered the prior reading level. There are many available books for children so parents can supply their child with endless topics and stories. Truly, there is something for every taste and interest.

In order to encourage their child to read, parents can place books at the child's eye level with the book's spine facing outward. Some children enjoy having their own reading area, tent, or corner. Some like to have their books in a family area where they can read while socializing. Some children are drawn to the e-readers. There are apps and toys that read *to* the child as the child follows along. Allowing a child to read for a while before bedtime is a relaxing way to end the day and prepare for sleep. Sometimes a preschooler will wake up early before it is acceptable to disturb the other family members. Allowing a child to read quietly in her room may be a reasonable solution to this family situation. Some preschoolers enjoy reading to their baby siblings, pets, stuffed animals, and dolls. Of course, it is especially fun for most children to read with their parents or grandparents. After considering the difficulty of the reading level of the selected book, the adult and child could take turns reading a page at a time. If the book is too long to finish in one sitting, the child could place a *personalized* bookmark at the stopping place.

When you read with your child, you can monitor your child's reading skills. If your child is mispronouncing the consonants, blends, or vowel sounds, you can help your child review those skills. (see Chapter 2) You can point out that sentences begin with a capital letter and end with a period (.), question mark (?), or exclamation point (!). (If your child knows these rules of grammar/reading, it will put a smile on every first grade teacher's face!) You can help your child with difficult vocabulary and introduce her to the *sight words* that are part of the curriculum of the early elementary school years. Here is a list of those words that do not follow the sound patterns that have already been discussed, but are essential that your child learns.

Sight Words

again	go	once	too
all	good	one	two
are	have	our	walk
away	he	out	want
be	here	round	was
brown	how	said	we
by	into	saw	were
come	know	say	what
could	live	so	when
do	look	some	where
down	me	soon	who
every	my	the	yellow
find	news	there	you
four	now	they	
from	of	to	

Most school districts prefer that their incoming kindergarteners have had exposure to words that rhyme. Here is yet another list of "words" that can be written on flashcards and used by the parents to benefit the child. The alphabetic consonants and the blends (see Chapter 2) can be coupled with the endings to make a variety of new words that the child can easily read. (Furthermore, I have used this technique to help my school-aged students pronounce multiple-syllable words. Exposing your preschooler to this activity can pay dividends for years to come.) If your preschooler does not read, this activity can be done verbally. Young children will enjoy this word-play game. Below is the list of common "word endings" that are extremely helpful to the novice reader.

Common Word Endings

__able	__each	__ick	__oat	__ug
__ack	__eak	__ift	__ock	__um
__ade	__ed	__ike	__oke	__ump
__ag	__eed	__ill	__ool	__un
__ail	__ell	__im	__oop	__unch
__ain	__en	__in	__oor	__up
__all	__end	__ine	__ord	__ust
__ame	__est	__ip	__orn	__ut

__an	__ew	__ipe	__ort
__ane	__it	__ot	
__ank	__ite		
__ast			
__at			
__ate			
__awl			
__ay			

Now let me show you an activity so you will know how to use this list to create a variety of rhyming words. Select a "word ending," perhaps *ine* or *im*. When the consonants and blends are added to the front of these letters, you can make words for simple poems. For example:

__ine		**__im**	
brine	shine	brim	slim
dine	shrine	dim	swim
fine	spine	grim	Tim
line	swine	him	trim
mine	twine	Jim	whim
nine	whine	Kim	
pine		prim	
vine		rim	
wine		skim	

Bobby Buttrey, who is nine,
Built a tree house in a pine.
Tied it on with lots of twine.
Now it is his favorite shrine.

or

My brother, Jim is very trim.
My neighbor, Kim is neatly prim.
But the new boy by the name of Tim,
Well, no one really knows about him.

There are other words that would rhyme with, but are not spelled like, the original endings. For example: *sign* (__ine) or *gym* (__im). I'm sure that you can think of others, too. Be creative and have fun with this word-play game. This will also give you a chance to increase your preschooler's vocabulary. You may have to explain the meaning of *skim* and *whim* or the difference between wine and whine.

Your child's vocabulary and understanding may be beyond her ability to actually read at the level that uses complex terms and ideas. This situation presents another perfect opportunity to read *to* your child. Challenge your child without overwhelming him. Some stories present a better read-out-loud experience than others when the flow of the story with its descriptions and word play are factored into the mix. Your local children's librarian can be extremely helpful to you by suggesting books that are "winners" in the read-aloud world. (Many libraries offer "story time" events where books are read to eager groups of preschoolers. Children's librarians offer a valuable source for read-aloud material.)

Here are some suggestions made by Paula M. Shadle, MLS, Children's Service Manager, Avon Lake Public Library, Avon Lake, Ohio.

Books to Enjoy Together

Beginning Readers
Disney	*Friends for a Princess (Step into Reading series)*
Rookie	*Balls (Rookie Reader series)*
Ruane	*Boats, Boats, Boats (My First Reader series)*
Schwartz	*Busy Buzzing Bumblebees and Other Tongue Twisters (an I Can Read Book series)*
Seuss	*Mr. Brown Can Moo! Can You?*
	The Foot Boot (Bright and Early Books for Beginning Readers series)
We	*The Frog Prince (We Both Read series)*
Ziefert	*The Magic Porridge Pot*

"Fun" Books
Ahlberg	*Each Peach Pear Plum*
Aronsky	*Rabbits and Raindrops*
Asch	*Moonbear's Dream*
Barrett	*Cloudy With a Chance of Meatballs*
Braun	*I Love My Mommy*
Bruce	*Fran's Flower*
Carle	*Mister Seahorse*
	The Very Hungry Caterpillar
Carr	*Frozen Noses*
Cauley	*Clap Your Hands*
Crews	*Freight Train*
Dunbar	*Baby Bird*
	The Very Small

Edwards	*Goodnight Baxter*
Ehlert	*Feathers for Lunch*
	Snowballs
Emmett	*Someone Bigger*
Falconer	*Olivia*
Faulkner	*The Big Yawn*
Feiffer	*Bark George*
Flemming	*Barnyard Banter*
	In the Tall, Tall Grass
Freymann	*Dog Food*
Gackenbach	*Claude the Dog*
	Claude Has a Picnic
George	*Into the Woods: Who's Been Here?*
Hindley	*Does a Cow Say Boo?*
Jorgensen	*Crocodile Beat*
	Gotcha!
Kalman	*What Pete Ate from A – Z*
Kasza	*The Wolf's Chicken Stew*
Kraus	*Mouse in Love*
Lavis	*Jump!*
Martin	*Brown Bear, Brown Bear, What Do You See?*
	Polar Bear, Polar Bear, What Do You Hear?
	Chicka Chicka Boom Boom
Mayhew	*Cluck, Cluck Who's There*
McGeorge	*Chestnut*
McMullen	*It's Too Soon*
Miranda	*To Market, To Market*
Most	*The Cow That Went Oink, Z-Z-Zoink*
Nelson	*Frosty the Snowman*
Numeroff	*If You Give a Mouse a Cookie*
Riley	*Mouse Mess*
Shelby	*Potluck*
Simmons	*Come Along, Daisy!*
Slobodkina	*Caps for Sale*
Small	*Imogene's Antlers*
Steig	*Which Would You Rather Be?*
Stoceke	*Minerva Louise*
	A Hat for Minerva Louise
Sturges	*I Love Trains*
Vagin	*The Enormous Carrot*
Walsh	*Mouse Paint*
Webb	*Tanka Tanka Skunk!*

Willems	*The Pigeon Finds a Hotdog*
Wood	*The Little Mouse*
	The Napping House
	The Red Ripe Strawberry and the Big Hungry Bear

Music

Archambault	*Chicka Chika Boom Boom and other Coconutty Songs*
Greg	*Greg & Steve Playing Favorites*
Palmer	*Can a Jumbo Jet Sing the Alphabet?*
Wee	*Wee Sing Games, Games, Games*

Nonfiction Favorites

Forest	*Stone Soup*
Gilman	*Something from Nothing*
Harper	*The Gunniwolf*
Katz	*Truck Talk*
Stille	*Fire Trucks*
Turnbull	*Trains*
Zemach	*The Three Wishes*

Repetition

Carlstrom	*Jesse Bear, What Will You Wear?*
Kalan	*Jump, Frog, Jump!*
Tafuri	*The Ball Bounced*

Rhyming Opposites

Dewdney	*Llama Llama Red Pajama*
Gordon	*Up Down*
Packard	*Same and Different*
Thompson	*Drat That Fat Cat*

Songs and Rhymes

Andreae	*Commotion in the Ocean*
Aylesworth	*Old Black Fly*
Baker	*The Big Fat Hen*
Birdseye	*She'll Be Comin' Round the Mountain*
Keats	*Over in the Meadow*
Raffi	*This Little Light of Mine*
Rebus	*Rebus Treasury*
Siomades	*The Itsy Bitsy Spider*
Whippo	*Little White Duck*
Winter	*The House*

Wood   Silly, Sally

Wordless Books
dePaola   *Pancakes for Breakfast*
Mayer   *A Boy, A Dog, and A Frog (series)*
Sis   *Beach Ball*

Resources for Parents & Caregivers
Barron   *Ready, Set, Read and Write*
Burns, Snow,
 and Griffin *Starting Out Right*
Corbell   *Scholastic Visual Dictionary*
Gillespi   *Best Books for Children Preschool Through Grade 6*
Hoberman   *You Read to Me, I'll Read to You*
Kingfisher *First Dictionary*
Lieberman *Kindersounds: Games*
Moomaw   *More Than Letters*

This resource list is a very good starting place to locate books that can be read to preschoolers in group settings or individually. However, there are other quality books that are available in local libraries and bookstores that will stimulate and delight your child also. Many libraries have printable booklists on their websites that will help parents select appropriate reading material for their toddlers. For example, parents will find the *Kindergarten Countdown: 100 Books to Read Before Kindergarten* on the Louisville Free Public Library website. (According to the website "The list was modified from the New York Public Library's *100 Picture Books Everyone Should Know*.") According to Mrs. Shadle, from the Avon Lake Public Library, Avon Lake, Ohio, "Lists like these are excellent sources for read-a-louds and for just plain 'good' books!"

The Take-Away
- Read to your infant so she hears the soothing tones of human speech
- Read to your baby to increase her working and listening vocabulary
- Read to your child so he will hear the grammar of his native language in context
- Read to your preschooler to broaden her experiences of life
- Read to your toddler to increase your child's interest in books and learning
- Read to your munchkin to capitalize on your child's readiness to learn and to monitor your child's reading skills
- Read to your toddler for the emotional closeness
- **Read to your child for the sheer fun of it!**

Techniques to Try

1. Point out the details within the pictures
2. Discuss categories: doggy's eyes, Shelley's eyes
3. Discuss relationships: doggy's paws are for walking, Shelley's feet are for walking
4. Point out the punctuation marks
5. Point out the capital letters
6. Tell your child that capital letters start a sentence and start a name
7. Discuss rhymes and opposites
8. Ask your child to find alphabet letters
9. Ask your child to tell the sounds that the letters make
10. Ask your child to find the numbers
11. Ask your child to count to that number
12. If the pages of the book are numbered, let your child find the right page
13. Give your child a bookmark with his/her name on it
14. Ask your child to find shapes and colors
15. Ask who is in the story
16. Ask what is happening in the story
17. Ask if there is a clue about where the story is happening
18. Ask if there is a clue about when the story is happening
19. Ask if anybody has a problem in the story
20. Ask if the problem got fixed
21. Ask how the problem got fixed
22. Read the neighborhood signs when you are out together
23. Make/buy flashcards of the alphabet, consonant blends, and vowels; flip and read them together
24. Make/buy flashcards of the sight words; flip and read them together
25. Make/buy flashcards of the common word endings; flip and read them together
26. Make up short verbal poems together; write them down for your child to read again later
27. Take your child to story hour at the library
28. Let your child choose his own library books to take home
29. Display the books at home at your child's eye level so she can see the book's spine
30. Set up a reading area or tent

Chapter Six

Prepare Your Preschooler for Science

Social Skills
- Follow three-step directions
- Complete a ten-minute activity with focus
- Attentively listen for a ten-minute period of time
- Respect and take care of personal belongings and those of others
- Show respect for and follow directions of those in authority
- Be able to take turns

Cognitive Skills
- Recognize most letters
- Recognize shapes, such as rectangle, square, triangle, and circle
- Identify objects and know their actions: a seed can grow a new plant
- Know colors
- Count to at least 20
- Have been exposed to written numerals 0-10
- Recognize directional words, such as in, out, up, and down
- Recognize comparison words, such as big, biggest, smaller, and larger
- Retell a familiar story

"Why" is a typical question of the developing toddler. Children want to understand how the world works and how things relate to each other. This desire to have a rational explanation seems to have no age limit. Learning involves having our world make sense.

Science is the discipline of discovery. The concepts of logic and reasoning (see Chapter 4) are food for the inquiring young mind. Young children use the powers of their five senses to experience their world. Parents can facilitate their child's understanding when they discuss the concepts of science during daily activities. For example, during a walk in the neighborhood, a child may notice ants or bees. If time permits, linger and watch the insects' activities for a while. Parents can discuss the value of such animals and their important relationship to the plants around them. On the same walk, perhaps a child notices the leaves that were green all summer are now red, orange, and yellow. This is not only a chance to review the names of the colors, but also a non-threatening opportunity to discuss photosynthesis. Use the term *photosynthesis*. Explain as much as you can remember about the process. Later, you can borrow a preschool-level library book on the topic and continue the science experience.

When you decorate your child's room, consider a mobile of the solar system, attach glow-in-the-dark constellations to the ceiling, or place an easy to read thermometer/barometer in your child's view. Use colorful placemats featuring a science theme such as the human skeleton and internal body organs, garden bugs and plants, or perhaps biomes of the planet.

With supervision a magnifying glass or a set of magnets could prove educational. You could try simple experiments together. Here are some easy, effective, ones for the busy parent:

1. Fill a glass about half full with water.
2. Add several drops of red food coloring.
3. Cut the bottom end from a large stalk of celery that still has some leaves on it.
4. Place the stalk of celery in the glass and leave it for seven to eight hours.

Your child will be surprised to see that the red food-colored water has entered the plant. You will be able to discuss *xylem* and *phloem*, and explain how tall trees and plants get a drink of water! (If you have to make a quick trip to the Internet, then you've learned something too. The longer I live, the more I realize how much I still have to learn!)

While you're on the topic of plants, why not try this easy activity?

1. Soak a folded paper towel.
2. Put a few uncooked lima beans or peas on the top of the wet towel, and place them in a zipper-locked sandwich bag so the seeds are visible.
3. Keep the seeds at room temperature: do not let the paper towel get dry.

Within days the seeds will sprout. You will get to talk about a plant's leaf and stem. When the stem has grown an inch long, your child can plant his sprout outside or in a flower pot, and continue to watch the plant develop.

This next activity will take all summer, but it is great fun for your child to plant a sunflower seed and to watch this fast growing plant reach tall heights. You might help your child measure the plant as it grows (about once a week should be fine), perhaps keep a growth chart, and ultimately feed the birds with the many, many seeds it produces by autumn!

In fact, why not feed the birds all winter? Seeds, bread, and suet will attract many varieties of birds. However, if you begin this activity, be sure to continue supplying food until the spring. The birds will count on this food source to sustain them. Hang your feeder so your child can enjoy the birds' activities as she plays or eats. You will be able to discuss kinds of birds, types of bird beaks, different bird calls, taking turns, counting, colors, size, etc. Maybe your feeder will also attract chipmunks, squirrels, a raccoon, or even a skunk. (Wait, this may *not* be such a good idea! Caution: Bird Feeders at Own Risk!)

Learning about their world delights most children. The wonder and excitement of your child will probably encourage you to do other science activities together. As you prepare your child for school, you can greatly expand the experience when you guide her through the process which actual scientists use, the *scientific method*: form a question/state a problem; make observations/collect data; guess what will happen/construct a hypothesis; do the experiment; draw a conclusion/decide if the experiment supported your original guess. Generally speaking, science attempts to understand our world. Furthermore, the discipline of science goes beyond simple observation and description. Scientists try to explain why things are the way they are and why things happen as they do.

As you begin an experiment, ask your child to guess or *hypothesize* about what she thinks might happen during the experiment. Do not tell your child what should happen, but let her *predict*, and ultimately, *discover* the outcome. You can now discuss how professional scientists predict, try, and maybe fail many times before they succeed. Often scientists learn only what doesn't work, but those are valuable lessons too.

The Take-Away
- Children love to understand their world
- Pull science topics into their daily lives through casual discussion, manipulative toys, experiments, outings, movies, and books
- When you discuss science or do experiments together, ask your child to predict a result and then let her discover the outcome

Techniques to Try

1. Discuss the concepts of science during daily activities
2. During a walk in the neighborhood, notice ants or bees
   a. Watch the insects' activities for a while
   b. Discuss the value of such animals and their important relationship to the plants around them
3. Notice the leaves that were green all summer are now red, orange, and yellow
   a. Review the names of the colors
   b. Discuss photosynthesis. Use the term photosynthesis. Explain as much as you can remember about the process. Later, you can borrow a preschool-level library book on the topic and continue the science experience
4. Decorate your child's room with a mobile of the solar system
5. Attach glow-in-the-dark constellations to the ceiling
6. Place an easy to read thermometer/barometer within your child's view
7. Use colorful placemats featuring a science theme such as the human skeleton and internal body organs, garden bugs and plants, or perhaps biomes of the planet
8. With supervision, use a magnifying glass or a set of magnets
9. Try simple experiments together
10. Discuss xylem and phloem, and explain how tall trees and plants get a drink of water
11. Plant a sunflower seed and watch this fast growing plant reach tall heights
    a. Measure the plant as it grows
    b. Keep a growth chart
12. Feed the birds
    a. Discuss kinds of birds, types of bird beaks, different bird calls, taking turns, counting, colors, and size
13. Guide your child through the experiment using the scientific method:
    a. Form a question/state a problem
    b. Make observations/collect data
    c. Guess what will happen/construct a hypothesis
    d. Do the experiment
    e. Draw a conclusion/decide if the experiment supported your original guess

Chapter Seven

Prepare Your Preschooler for Social Studies

Social Skills
- Follow three-step directions
- Complete a ten-minute activity with focus
- Attentively listen for a ten-minute period of time
- Respect and take care of personal belongings and those of others
- Show respect for and follow directions of those in authority
- Be able to take turns

Cognitive Skills
- Recognize own name in print
- Recognize most letters
- Know own birth date, phone number, and address
- Recognize shapes, such as rectangle, square, triangle, and circle
- Identify objects and know their actions (a map shows a flat surface of a place)
- Know colors
- Count to at least 20
- Have been exposed to written numerals 0-10
- Recognize directional words, such as in, out, up, and down
- Recognize comparison words, such as big, bigger, biggest, smaller, and larger
- Retell a familiar story

"Grammy, tell me what Mama did when she was three years old."

"Grandpa, did you have a computer when you were five, like me?"

"Uncle Jim, how do you know the way to get to my house?"

"Daddy, where does that river go?"

"Mommy, can we look at the old pictures again?"

Real people, real places, and real events are interesting to children. When your child asks questions like these, you have an opportunity to talk about the concepts that will prepare him for school. Social studies tells stories about real people, places, and events. Social studies explains community, ancestry, neighborhood, customs, culture, population, citizenship, geography, resources, history, climate, government, and map skills.

Schools recommend that incoming kindergarteners know their addresses. While you're teaching your child this important fact, and answering his questions presented above, why not seize the opportunity to discuss other social studies-related concepts?

While you are running errands or taking a walk, you can describe the neighborhood and community. Name the streets and point out the landmarks, especially if you travel that route often. Don't be surprised if your child incorporates these exact street names and places into her play. Draw a crude map of your community on a large piece of cardboard, and label the streets and landmarks. Let your child drive her cars and trucks on this "map." Another option is to use permanent marker pens to draw roads and landmarks on a large white vinyl picnic tablecloth. The tablecloth map can be folded for easy storage.

Colorful world maps make great wall hangings for bedrooms or play areas. Puzzles featuring the country with the individual states (or provinces) teach geography, as well as help develop those small motor muscles in the hands. These puzzles help children recognize each state by shape as the children orient the puzzle pieces for proper fit. Preschoolers may even learn to read the names of the states along the way! Some puzzles are interactive and recite the *Pledge of Allegiance* and play patriotic songs. Furthermore, map reading skills can be introduced at a very young age if the terms *north/south* and *east/west* are added to your child's list of opposites. No doubt, preschoolers hear these words anyway whenever the GPS is used while driving.

Mealtime is a wonderful opportunity to stimulate your child educationally. Normally the toddler wears a seatbelt or has learned to remain seated during the meal. This affords parents or caregivers time to interact with the child in an attention-focused way. Topics can vary depending upon the amount of time available, but some of this time can be used for social studies rich content. For example, you could chat about family customs and ancestry, cultures in other lands, national heritage, or the steps of how the child's food got from the farm to the table. If your child uses a placemat, find some with a social studies theme. Perhaps you could find one featuring the government monuments and buildings of Washington, D.C. (White House, Jefferson Memorial, National Gallery of Art, the Capitol, Washington Monument, Supreme Court Building,

Smithsonian Institution, Lincoln Memorial, etc.) Buy placemats that feature neighborhood traffic road signs, all of the presidents, an enlarged map of your state or city, the world's time zones, or a map of the world's hemispheres. (You may think that these topics are too advanced for a child so young, but toddlers and preschoolers remind me of the character ET from the movie with the same name. ET was constantly asking for "more input.") Exposure to these terms with a rudimentary understanding of the context is really all that is needed at this point. If your child is interested in exploring the content further, you can always expand on the individual topic or seek additional resources. If your toddler is "gifted," your child will really enjoy this additional mental stimulation.

Children enjoy marching and dancing to music. What do you think would happen if your child heard the patriotic marches of John Phillips Sousa or the songs of the Navy, Army, Air Force, Marine Corps, and Coast Guard? YouTube not only plays the songs, but has exciting pictures to accompany the music. You could also treat your child to music of all cultures and religions. Then, using a world map, show your child where the people from those cultures live.

Observe the national holidays like Martin Luther King, Jr. Day, Presidents' Day, Memorial Day, Flag Day, Independence Day, Labor Day, Columbus Day, Election Day, Veterans Day, and others of your choosing so you can mention the history or significance of the date. Remember, this is not a lecture. This is exposure and an invitation to learn more now and later. Observe or celebrate the social and religious holidays to teach culture and customs. Simple decorations or special foods can be the beginning of understanding these special dates. Perhaps your preschooler can help decorate or help prepare some of the food. These are perfect times to chat with each other about the festivities. In addition, the mention and observation of the first days of spring, summer, autumn, and winter can reinforce the concepts of social studies, as well as science. In fact, why not watch the weather report together. Your child can broaden his world as he understands the communities surrounding his home.

When you visit a zoo or a museum, show your child the homeland of the snowy owl, zebra, and Indian elephant. Use the map to locate where the dinosaur bones were found. Borrow library book so you can read stories about the geography of the natural habitat of the zoo animals or about the dinosaurs that lived long ago.

Use the library as a resource for stories about famous people. The children's section has many wonderful short biographies about our national heroes and other world personalities. You can sprinkle in a little Abe Lincoln and Ben

Franklin among the tiny tadpoles and bouncy bunnies of the child's literary realm.

The Take-Away

• You will expand your child's knowledge of social studies content through casual discussion, manipulative toys, trips while doing normal daily errands, music, decorations, movies, and books

• Remember, these teaching opportunities are used to *expose* your child to the social studies concepts, and to *invite* your child to learn more about the subject now and later

Techniques to Try

1. Teach your child his/her name, address, and phone number
2. Describe the neighborhood or community while running errands or taking a walk
3. Name the streets
4. Point out the landmarks
5. Draw a map of your community on cardboard so your child can drive her cars and trucks on its surface
6. Use permanent marker pens to draw roads and landmarks on a large white vinyl picnic tablecloth so your child can drive his cars and trucks on its surface
7. Draw circles, triangles, squares, and rectangles on these "maps" to represent the landmarks
8. Watch the weather report together and notice the maps
9. Hang colorful maps as wall hangings in your child's bedroom or play area.
10. Play with puzzles featuring the country with the individual states or provinces
11. Recite the *Pledge of Allegiance*
12. Play patriotic music
13. Introduce the terms *north/south* and *east/west* into your child's list of opposites
14. Chat with your child about family customs and ancestry
15. Talk about cultures in other lands
16. March, skip, hop, or dance to the music of other cultures and religions
17. Mention national heritage
18. Observe and discuss the history and the significance of the national holidays
19. Observe and discuss the social and religious holidays to teach culture and customs
20. Explain the steps of how the child's food got from the farm to the table
21. Use placemats that feature a social studies theme
22. Let your preschooler help you decorate or serve special foods to begin your child's understanding of these special dates (national holidays, religious and cultural holidays)
23. Mention or observe the first days of spring, summer, autumn, and winter
24. Visit a zoo or a museum
25. Show your child the homeland of the zoo animals
26. Borrow books from the library with a social studies theme
27. Read short biographies about our national heroes or world personalities which are available from the children's section of the library

Chapter Eight

Prepare Your Preschooler for Math

Physical Skills
- Hold and use scissors and pencils correctly
- Work neatly using glue, scissors, pencils, and crayons
- Copy shapes and letters
- Hold a book correctly
- Build with blocks

Social Skills
- Follow three-step directions
- Complete a ten-minute activity with focus
- Attentively listen for a ten-minute period of time
- Respect and take care of personal belongings and those of others
- Show respect for and follow directions of those in authority
- Be able to take turns

Cognitive Skills
- Know own birth date, phone number, and address
- Recognize shapes, such as rectangle, square, triangle, and circle
- Identify objects and know their actions (example: calendar counts time)
- Know colors
- Count to at least 20
- Have been exposed to written numerals 0-10
- Have been exposed to rhymes and opposites
- Recognize directional words, such as in, out, up, and down
- Recognize comparison words, such as big, bigger, biggest, smaller, and larger

In, on, under . . . you may be checking the chapter's title soon. Is this really a math chapter? Those are prepositions. This seems like a grammar topic. Nope, math!

Math Vocabulary for Preschoolers
Preschoolers will learn math concepts more easily if they understand the meaning of these prepositions:

about	behind	from	past

above	below	in	through
across	beneath	into	to
after	beside	like	toward
against	between	near	under
along	beyond	of	until
among	by	off	up
around	down	on	with
at	during	out	within
before	for	over	without

Preschoolers will understand math better if they know the meaning of these adjectives:

big	fewer	little	short
different	full	long	similar
empty	heavy	more	symmetrical
equal	light	same	tall

These addition and subtraction clues will help preschoolers understand story problems.

Addition		Subtraction	
add	more	decrease	more than
altogether	plus	difference	opposite
gain	sum	fewer than	subtract
in all	tax	left	take away
increase	together	lose	words that compare:
join	total	minus	older/taller/younger

Introduce your child to words that measure time:

calendar	season
clock	second
day	today
hour	tomorrow
minute	week days
month	year
now	yesterday

Expose your child to words that measure weight and length:

Liquid	Solid	Length
ounce	ounce	inch
cup	pound	foot
pint	ton	yard

quart	gram	mile
half-gallon		meter
gallon		
liter		

These terms will help your child understand geometry:

triangle	circle
square	oval
parallelogram	star
rectangle	point
rhombus	line
trapezoid	plane
pentagon	angle
hexagon	straight
heptagon	curve
decagon	

Preschoolers will understand money if you talk about:

penny
nickel
dime
quarter
half-dollar
dollar

Talk to your preschooler using these terms of fractions:

eighths
sixths
quarters
thirds
halves
whole

Initially, your child will probably understand the concept of numbers via discovering his fingers and toes. Later, playing board games will give your child practice counting, as well as adding money or the markings on dice. In the meantime, you can help your child earn success in math by familiarizing him with the previously stated vocabulary terms. Simply by emphasizing these terms in your daily conversation with your child, you will be instilling the essence of math concepts which are taught in more detail in school. The math curriculum requirements have intensified. Many of these concepts are introduced to children at much lower grade levels than they were when I first began teaching. Here are some of the concepts which your young child will encounter within the first few years of school:

- Counting numerals
- Reading numerals
- Writing numerals
- Ordering numerals
- Understanding the value of numbers
- Locating numbers on a number line
- Counting forwards and backwards
- Recognizing number words
- Understanding one-to-one correspondence (7 snowman, 7 hats—each snowman has a hat)
- Identifying curved and straight lines
- Recognizing and naming shapes
- Drawing or finding shapes in real life
- Measuring
- Comparing sizes
- Finding and continuing patterns
- Estimating
- Saying the names of the days of the week, the months of the year, and the seasons (in order)
- Reading a calendar
- Sequencing numbers (1st, 2nd, 3rd, 4th, 5th)
- Understanding fractions
- Recognizing coins
- Understanding the value of a penny, a nickel, a dime, and a quarter
- Reading analog and digital clocks
- Understanding the concept of addition
- Understanding the concept of subtraction
- Recognizing the symbols +, -, =
- Understanding the concept of zero

My forty years of teaching experience has influenced my thinking regarding calculation vs. concept. Calculation takes place when a student applies the rules for the arithmetic. (For example, a student must remember to make the denominators of fractions common before adding or subtracting the numerators of the fractions. However, common denominators are not necessary when—blah, blah, blah.) If a student knows the rules for this calculation, a student can perform the calculations accurately without understanding the concepts associated with fractions, or for that matter, where these calculations would be useful in practical, everyday life! Math calculations involve remembering and applying many rules. Children are often frustrated when they try to deal with so much detail. On the other hand, calculation can become easier, even intuitive, when students understand the concepts that logically suggest the arithmetic.

I've learned that students have their own ways of processing information, and that thinking works better when the individual has some control. I've tutored hundreds of students who have gradually discovered how they personally process and use information. They develop their unique ways of organizing, studying, taking notes, managing their time, and juggling the other commitments in their lives when they are encouraged to reason and to problem-solve. It is my professional opinion that the earlier a child is encouraged to understand mathematical concepts the easier it will be for the child to perform mathematical calculation. Introducing your child to the vocabulary of math is the initial step. Later encourage your child to think logically, stressing math categories (ex: things that are big), relationships (ex: the number five comes between the numbers four and six), classifications (ex: pennies, nickels, dimes, and quarters look different from each other), associations (ex: if tricycles have three wheels and triangles have three sides, then tri must mean three), symbols (ex: "10" means all of my fingers), and pictures (ex: cut your child's sandwich or pancake into fourths and encourage your child to reassemble it on his plate before eating it).

The Take-Away
- The concepts of math involve understanding and using the vocabulary of comparing and contrasting
- Math groups items into categories and sets
- Children will need to learn to recognize and write the symbols for numbers, addition, subtraction, and equals in order to work with the concepts of math taught in the early elementary school years

Techniques to Try
1. Count the stairs as you go up and down
2. Count the traffic lights on the way to the store
3. Count the buttons on your child's shirt
4. Count the beads on the abacus
5. Count by ones
6. Count by fives
7. Count by tens
8. Count the numbers on the calendar
9. Have your child point to each item before saying the number

10. Read the numbers on signs and license plates
11. While taking a walk, read the addresses on houses
12. While reading, let your child read the page numbers
13. While reading, let your child find the page number that you name
14. Hold up a numbered flashcard and let your child draw that number in the air
15. While giving a back rub, write a number with your finger on your child's back and let her guess what number you wrote
16. Let your child "write" a number, letter, or shape using her finger on your back
17. Make numbers with clay
18. Write numbers with your finger in the sandbox or on the beach
19. Arrange magnetic numbers in numerical order
20. Using the computer let your child choose a large font and color so she can type the numbers in sequential order on a blank screen. Help her type higher and higher numbers
21. Match written numeral flashcards with numeric flashcards (one, 1; two, 2)
22. Enjoy a math workbook for preschoolers
23. Borrow library books about numbers
24. Arrange numbered flashcards in numerical order and place toys next to each card to represent the number on the flashcard (#3—place three dolls next to that card)
25. Let your child enjoy a dot-to-dot puzzle book
26. Have your child count backwards as she eats each spoonful of lunch
27. Count a line of popcorn and subtract one after your child eats each kernel
28. Play addition or subtraction games on the computer or apps
29. Place five toys in a bag. Remove two. Ask your child how many toys are left in the bag
30. Give your child two carrot sticks. Then give him three more carrot sticks. Ask him how many he has now. Ask him to make sure by counting the carrot sticks
31. Introduce your child to the concept of *zero*: say, "You ate all of your cookies. The cookies are gone. You have zero cookies."
32. After her bath let your child watch as the water drains out of the tub. Say, "There is zero water left in the bathtub."
33. Set a small table with dishes for a doll tea party. Give each doll the same number of dishes (one-to-one correspondence)
    a. Divide each doll's food portion equally (fractions)
34. Let your child pack the favors for his birthday party. Each guest will get the same items in each treat bag

35. Find pictures that show sets of dishes, sets of keys, and groups of children
36. Tell your child that you cut his sandwich in half or into fourths
37. Use shape sorter "cookie cutters" to make shapes in clay
38. Cut the clay shapes into halves, thirds, quarters, sixths, and eighths
39. Roll large, medium, and small balls of clay. Have your child arrange them from largest to smallest
40. Play a game of "Find-a-Shape." Name a shape, or hold up a shape flashcard, and have your child find an example of that shape in your house (rectangle—window; circle—doorknob)
41. Hunt for examples of curved and straight lines in your home
42. Draw shapes in the air
43. Look for shapes while taking a walk
44. Make patterns using shapes or colored beads. Let your child copy the pattern
45. Make patterns using shapes or colored beads. Let your child place the next several shapes/colored beads in your sequence
46. On a piece of paper, draw a red line, followed by a blue line, followed by a yellow line. If that pattern continued, ask your child to name the colored line that should be in the fifth position or row
47. Let your child make a necklace using 10 red beads, 10 blue beads, 10 yellow beads, and 10 green beads
48. Using colored blocks, make patterns such that the same colors do not touch each other
49. Place number stickers on your child's toys and let him "buy" the toys with the correct number of pennies
50. Select four stuffed toys or dolls. Make a line of *first, second, third,* and *fourth*
51. Write the words *first, second, third, fourth,* etc. on a piece of paper. Let your child cut out the words and glue them to another paper in sequential order
52. Let your child count the coins in your pocket
53. Make play money with your child
54. Let your child pretend that his stuffed toys have favorite colors. Write the names of the colors on a piece of paper, and let your child make tally marks to keep track of the stuffed toys' answers
55. Measure your child's height on a wall chart which is within your child's view
56. Roll clay "worms" and measure them with a ruler
57. Give your child measuring cups and a pail of water. Let him measure the water as he moves it from one container to the other
58. Let your child measure uncooked macaroni in the measuring cups

59. When cleaning up the toys, ask your child to guess how long it will take to put everything away (estimation)
60. While getting dressed, ask your child to guess how many socks are in the drawer. Then count them
61. Have your child make a new calendar each month by writing the numbers on the correct days
    a. Have your child place the name of the month and the days of the week on his calendar
    b. Have your child place family birthdays and holidays on his calendar
62. Place a digital and an analog clock in your child's bedroom, eating area, or play area
63. Read the time on the clock to your child frequently during the day.
    a. Say, "We are eating lunch at 11:00."
    b. Say, "We need to get ready for bed by 7:30."
64. Tell your child that he has to brush his teeth for two minutes. Then set a timer so he can understand how long two minute takes
65. Move your child's favorite stuffed toys *between* the blocks, *above* the table, *under* the chair, *in* the box
    a. Using those same stuffed toys or dolls, ask your child which is the biggest and smallest
66. When looking at pictures of farm or jungle animals, ask your child which animal's ears are long/short, which animal is tall/short, or which animal is heavy/light
67. Think of other ways to teach the vocabulary list at the beginning of this math chapter
68. Point to items in your home that have symmetry
69. Introduce numbers to 100
70. Introduce simple addition and subtraction facts

Chapter Nine

Prepare Your Preschooler for the Rigors of the School Day

Physical Skills
- Independently take care of toilet needs
- Self-dress: tie shoes, button, snap, zip
- Hold and use scissors and pencils correctly
- Work neatly using glue, scissors, pencils, and crayons
- Copy shapes and letters
- Hold a book correctly
- Build with blocks
- Catch and throw a ball
- Stand on one foot, skip, gallop, jump, and hop

Social Skills
- Follow three-step directions
- Complete a ten-minute activity with focus
- Attentively listen for a ten-minute period of time
- Respect and take care of personal belongings and those of others
- Show respect for and follow directions of those in authority
- Be able to take turns

Cognitive Skills
- Recognize own name in print
- Write own name
- Recognize most letters
- Know own birth date, phone number, and address
- Recognize shapes, such as rectangle, square, triangle, and circle
- Identify objects and know their actions (example: scissors cut paper)
- Know colors
- Count to at least 20
- Have been exposed to written numerals 0-10
- Have been exposed to rhymes and opposites
- Recognize directional words, such as in, out, up, and down
- Recognize comparison words, such as big, bigger, biggest, smaller, and larger
- Retell a familiar story

A parent's job . . . to raise a child or to raise an adult? If you choose the latter, you'll need to stress independence. Babies and toddlers are inexperienced in social interaction. Preparing your preschooler for the rigors of the school day involves helping your child practice social skills. Successful social interaction requires cooperation, sharing, and sensitivity to the needs of others, as well as understanding the feelings and thoughts of others. Relating well to one's peers involves making positive comments and helpful suggestions. Teaching your child appropriate social awareness will help your child be accepted by his/her peers.

Babies and toddlers must navigate beyond their self-centeredness to understand other points of view. This transition gradually develops between the ages of three and five as the child's awareness of the world grows. Preschoolers see the world from the perspective of their own wants and needs. The young child may think that everyone feels, sees, and wants exactly what he feels, sees, and wants. Parents must help their child transition from this concrete thinking to more abstract reasoning.

Babies are interested in each other. They stare, lean forward as if to get a closer look, and often move their arms, legs, and heads with excitement. They might show each other a toy, or perhaps they will use grunts or partial words to request something. Babies may protest another's actions or get very excited when offered what they understand, like a bath or a doll. Toddlers may copy the movements of a peek-a-boo game or of an itsy-bitsy spider. Toddlers may often run after one another. Preschoolers show lots of social interest in their peers!

Between the ages of six and eight, most children realize that others have different perspectives but think that everyone possesses the same information. Children in the lower elementary grades tend to judge another's actions from their own perspective, and cannot see themselves as others do.

Children between the ages of eight and ten can understand that individual differences are based upon a person's basic values. In fact, another's goals can differ too. Children of these ages can predict another person's reactions, and they can analyze how their own behavior could affect someone else.

By the time children enter their teenage years, they are able to examine their own behavior and point of view, as well as those of others. Teenagers can analyze, predict, evaluate, imagine, compare and contrast, and understand the philosophical content of an argument. Their thinking is definitely on a higher plane.

So, how do parents get their child from zero to teen? How do parents foster the qualities of concern for others that will help their child "work and play well with others," so their child will be able to relate to individual friends and the peer group as a whole? Fortunately, children learn to share, to cooperate, and to imagine themselves in the roles of others and to curb their impulses for immediate gratification through *play*.

Children benefit physically, emotionally, and intellectually while playing. They exercise their large and small muscles, occupy themselves, and develop skills that are necessary for functioning as adults. Through movement, children realize that they are separate from other people and have freedom to control some functions of their lives. They may play with their fingers and feet, experiment with making sounds, bang every object they pick up on the table—or suck on it—and begin to explore their surroundings when they are able to crawl and walk. Children can be powerful when they become the big, strong monster during fantasy play or they can be in control of their environment when they play with miniature toys. Who hasn't watched a child feed all of the stuffed animal friends, or play with a small kitchen set or a child-sized carpenter's toolbox? Children dress up and pretend to be astronauts, super heroes, or characters from their favorite storybooks. Play can also be an intellectual activity. Perhaps a child has learned how to operate the TV remote. After manipulating the device for a time or two, the child can set channels, stop and start movies, and even program the remote to record a program for later viewing!

A baby's first social play experiences are probably with the parents or caregiver. A game of peek-a-boo or clapping hands can be a bonding event for a baby. Parents should encourage play which advances perceptual awareness, coordination, and encourages the social use of language. Later parents can initiate a game of tossing a ball back and forth, climbing a playground ladder, marching to music, or jumping to stimulate the large motor muscles. Stringing beads, drawing with crayons and chalk, painting, or cutting with scissors will stimulate the small motor muscles. Teaching these skills to your child will definitely help prepare your toddler for the rigors of the school day.

As the toddler matures, the child's social group of peers will also increase. The need for more cooperation and interaction between children presents more opportunities to practice the social skills. Playing with someone else involves taking turns. ("I'll let you use my truck, if I can play with yours.") Perhaps children will team up to build a block town. ("You build the houses, and I'll put out the train set.") If the group of children decides to play town, then all of the children will have to assume their roles. We don't need any monsters or pirates at this event! Now the children are practicing the social skills of cooperation, sharing, taking turns, and making constructive suggestions.

The parents' role in their child's play is sometimes direct. They actively engage their child: "Let's play with these blocks together, Ryne." Sometimes the parents offer oversight. This gives the child security and encouragement as he explores the environment and gains self-confidence in his social interactions with other peers. Wise parents give their child diverse experiences within the community. Your child will benefit from outings that expose him to the zoo, the park, the beach, the grocery store, the veterinarian's office, the post office, the library, the playground, etc. Sometimes the purpose of the outing could be strictly for socialization. Take your child to a restaurant. Help him to practice his "quiet" voice in this social setting, encourage him to be patient as he waits for the meal, and help him to stay seated until everyone has finished eating. If your child becomes disruptive, remove him from the restaurant. Perhaps you could sit in the car together, but do not play with him or make the removal "fun." Return to the setting when your child regains his composure. Teaching your child the accepted behavior for different venues will help your child be accepted and approved by others. (Another helpful book which I highly recommend is *Alyeska's Axioms for Parents, Child-Rearing Wisdom from My Dog* by Joyce Meagher, RN, LPC, LMFT, RPT-S.)

Read stories to your child in which the characters engage in social interaction with each other. These stories can help your child gain social and moral awareness. You can talk to your child about how the book's characters understand the feelings of one another. Choose stories that will help your child understand friendship and the welfare of others. Perhaps you need to help your child deal with negative feelings such as anger, jealousy, disappointment, sadness, and worry.

Children experience feelings that can overwhelm them. Emotions can affect any of us at any time, so we need to learn how to cope. Let's say your child is anxious about an upcoming dental appointment. She has never been to the dentist before and she is really quite worried. You could select a library book about Alex's first trip to the dentist. Alex—and your daughter—could learn about the dentist's chair, the bright light, the patient's bib, and the dentist's tools. Your daughter may ask you to read the book to her several times before her appointment. You have now prepared your child for her first dental visit because you have lessened her anxiety.

Adults have adult coping skills—and even those don't help in every circumstance. Consider how the feelings of young children can cause havoc. When your child observes the way the characters in stories are dealing with their emotions, your child will gain some personal insight too. It is a great opportunity for you to discuss successful social interaction.

Role-playing is another technique that helps children cope and learn social awareness. You could assume a role and let your child practice how to react. Perhaps you could role-play a person interrupting a conversation or speaking to an elderly neighbor. Role-play what to do if the doorbell rings or who to call if there is a fire or an accident. Your child may not have encountered these problems . . . yet. In the home you can help your child briefly explore some difficult social interactions, and then return to the reality of their secure setting. Let's say that you pretend to be a bully. Role-playing can be versatile, and the roles can be easily reversed to give your child the experience of being both the victim and the bully. The experience of being on both sides of the situation will give your child perspective from two points of view.

Successful social interaction is key to preparing your child for the rigors of the school day. It is not always enough for a child to simply have special attention from a caring adult in the home. Training in the social skills is needed too. This proficiency leads to a greater degree of peer acceptance. Well-liked children exhibit cooperative play, make social conversation, and give constructive suggestions. On the other hand, disliked children often make inappropriate or unrelated statements when conversing, or they make negative comments without offering constructive alternatives. Many disliked children are easily distracted and highly emotional. They can display antisocial, aggressive behavior and may be impulsive, self-centered, or immature. They can be disruptive, angry, and often retaliatory when in a group. The rejection that they ultimately feel from their peers may cause low self-esteem issues, depression, and foster an inability to be able to initiate future social contact.

Aggression can follow frustration. Aggression that is rewarded invites further aggressive behavior. Studies have shown that parents who are dealing with a child displaying aggression may be too permissive. The parents make few demands for positive social behavior. They may be lax in their supervision or inconsistent when disciplining their child. Instead of dealing harsh punishments, parents might:
1. Insist that the aggressor does something nice for the victim: "Since you hit your sister, you will have to pick up her half of the playroom today."
2. Encourage children to imagine how the victim feels: "Think about how Amy felt when you pinched her. Pretend you just got pinched (pause a second); what are your feelings?"
3. Teach your child to use his words to express his displeasure instead of

using physical acts such as hitting: "That makes me angry," or "Don't take my toy, Danny."

4. Explain to the aggressor: "Your baby brother is too young to know that he shouldn't take your toy, Marty, so you shouldn't punish him by punching him." Then parents have to teach baby brother, too! Parents can view these situations as teaching opportunities.

Social rejection and academic difficulties are often related. What might begin as antisocial behavior or being anxious while in class may snowball into poor grades from the child's inability to focus in an arena where he feels hostility. If the academic failure is related to social problems, then tutoring in academics can improve the child's social status. (I have tutored many children during my career who have found balance in both academics and peer acceptance.) Appropriate adult intervention works and offers hope to children experiencing the pain of social isolation.

Let me close this chapter with a few words about the gifted child. The precocious child is ahead of those in his chronological age group. Academically, the gifted child understands concepts easily, uses an extended vocabulary, and probably can already read. However, the gifted preschooler may be on par with his peer group when social awareness and social interactions are factored into the mix. The parents of the precocious child need to consider their child's ability to successfully interact with other children and help their child develop the social skills that are needed when attending school.

The Take-Away

- Coach your child in specific social and academic skills that are necessary for peer acceptance such as sharing, cooperation, initiating friendships, and making conversation
- Practice relating to others
- Encourage activities which foster greater self-awareness
- Participate in group games and activities
- Intervene when your child needs direction
- Help your child gain social perspective by placing your preschooler in actual social situations, by reading to your child, and by using role-playing exercises
- Helping your child gain successful social skills will indeed help prepare your child for the rigors of the school day

Techniques to Try

1. Begin reading story books to your toddler about using the potty
   a. Pretend that your child's favorite doll or stuffed animal friend is using the potty
   b. Introduce your child to the potty
2. Offer two appropriate outfits and let your child choose one he would like to wear
3. Encourage your child to dress himself independently until he needs your help
4. Let your child practice how to tie, button, snap, and zip items that she isn't wearing at the time
5. Demonstrate how to hold scissors and pencils correctly
6. Let your child cut, glue, color, paint, and scribble
7. Practice copying shapes and letters
8. String beads and draw with crayons or chalk
9. Let your child orient the book when you cuddle up to read together
10. Give your child a three-step direction to follow:
    a. Say, "Give Daddy the blue truck, the soft blanket, and the smallest ball."
    b. Say, "Take off your shoes, wash your hands, and get your snack in the refrigerator."
11. Guide your child to complete a ten-minute activity with focus:
    a. Say, "I'm going to set the kitchen timer, and we will practice our sight words until the buzzer rings."
12. Guide your child to attentively listen for a ten-minute period of time:
    a. Say, "I'm going to set the kitchen timer and let's listen to the birds at the bird feeder until the buzzer rings."
    b. Say, "Let's name all the instruments we hear in this music until the buzzer rings."
13. Help your child respect and take care of personal belongings and those of others:
    a. Say, "Put all of the pieces of your game away so you don't lose any. It won't be much fun to play the game if you don't have all of the pieces."
    b. Say, "These are Mommy's work papers, but I'll give you some paper where you can draw your shapes."
14. Help your child show respect for and follow directions of those in authority:
    a. Say, "Let's put your whines in your pocket. It really is time to clean up your toys for today."

15. Encourage your baby to mimic your actions: clap your hands, play peek-a-boo, hit two blocks together
16. Mimic the actions of your child. Play a game of *I'll Do What You Do*
17. Roll a ball back and forth
18. Take your child to the playground
19. March to music
20. Encourage your child to build with blocks
21. Catch and throw a ball to each other
22. Demonstrate how to stand on one foot, skip, gallop, jump, and hop
23. Invite your child to copy your actions
24. Toss a bean bag into a box
25. Make a play-date with a neighbor or friend
26. Let you child play dress-up
27. Play a preschool matching or board game together
28. Take your child on an outing for the experience and to teach appropriate social behavior
29. Read stories about values, social interactions, and morals
30. Role-play to help your child learn about social awareness and to practice coping skills

Chapter Ten

Important Toys for Play

Physical Skills
- Copy shapes and letters
- Hold a book correctly
- Build with blocks
- Catch and throw a ball
- Stand on one foot, skip, gallop, jump, and hop

Social Skills
- Follow three-step directions
- Complete a ten-minute activity with focus
- Attentively listen for a ten-minute period of time
- Respect and take care of personal belongings and those of others
- Show respect for and follow directions of those in authority
- Be able to take turns

Cognitive Skills
- Recognize own name in print
- Write own name
- Recognize most letters
- Recognize shapes, such as rectangle, square, triangle, and circle
- Identify objects and know their actions (example: scissors cut paper)
- Know colors
- Count to at least 20
- Have been exposed to written numerals 0-10
- Have been exposed to rhymes and opposites
- Recognize directional words, such as in, out, up, and down
- Recognize comparison words, such as big, bigger, biggest, smaller, and larger
- Retell a familiar story

The child's work is PLAY. Children engage in play because they want to; force is not a component of play. Children find the act of play pleasurable. They initiate the activity themselves, and they become psychologically and physically involved in their pursuit. Playful activities are often creative. Play can include other people or be done by the child alone. It can represent realistic behaviors such as several children riding their trikes up to a barrier which represents a toll-booth and paying the fare for exiting the "turnpike." Also play can be make-believe. Perhaps bath towels are safety pinned to the back of a child's garments to flap like the royal cape of a king or a queen. Play can be organized into the rules of a board game in which a child must have an understanding of counting, color, cooperation, or turn-taking, to name a few. Sometimes play can involve games of physical skill, such as electronic games, target toss games, or tricycle riding.

When a child uses his own ideas, problem solving occurs. Toys that run on the child's power such as a plain wooden car without a battery or a simple hand-puppet are some of the most useful toys. Children are naturally curious. They are eager to learn and succeed. They are proud of their accomplishments. Children are empowered when they are encouraged to think and to problem solve.

Great toys have a variety of uses, and they help children develop:
- Spatial skills
- Hand-eye coordination
- Large and fine motor skills
- Imagination
- Problem-solving skills
- Logical thinking
- A desire to explore their environment

Children benefit from playing with active toys and real items such as measuring spoons or an old wind-up clock. As children develop, they will find other uses for these toys which I would consider *staples*. Is there a place for the video games, other electronic devices, and toys with all the lights, bells, and whistles? Of course, but toys do not have to be expensive in order to stimulate a child. A preschooler can happily play with a common cardboard box, an old purse, or kitchen containers and utensils for long periods of time in many different ways. Give your child any one of these items and observe creativity and discovery in its purest form.

The Take-Away
- Learning occurs when a child uses his own ideas
- The most useful toys are operated by the child
- Toys that can be used in a variety of ways can be used differently by the child as she grows

Toys to Try

When choosing toys, get some *staples*:

1. Balls
2. Pull toys
3. Rattles
4. Bath toys
5. Sandbox toys
6. Animal characters (zoo, farm, jungle, etc.)
7. Dollhouses
8. Stuffed animals
9. Dolls
10. Hand puppets
11. Action figures
12. Trains
13. Cars and truck vehicles
14. Pattern blocks
15. Shape sorters
16. Puzzles
17. Abacuses
18. Latch boards
19. Blocks
20. Nesting cups
21. Toy food
22. Toy keys
23. Toy phones
24. Child-size brooms and lawn mowers
25. Dress-up clothes
26. Musical instruments
27. Matching and memory games
28. Board games
29. Magnetic alphabet letters/numbers
30. Child scissors (left-handed scissors for left-handed child)
31. Clay
32. Art supplies
33. Books
34. Child-size table and chairs
35. Wagons
36. Riding toys (tricycle, rocking horse, etc.)

Afterword

Newborn infants are born helpless, but lots of developmental changes take place during a child's early years. The learning curve for a human being is quite impressive. Babies, toddlers, and preschoolers have very special issues as they grow. I wrote this prequel to *Teach Your Child to Learn* in order to address these special issues and to explain to parents that they have a unique opportunity and privilege to watch and to participate in their child's maturation. The parents' involvement can have a positive influence on their young. In addition, they enhance their own lives too. Parents are their child's first teachers, and they can motivate their child to succeed BEFORE the child enters kindergarten.

You will soon hear your child say, "I did it!"

You will soon hear yourself say, "I'm having fun, too!"

About the Author

Since 1971 I've taught children and adults, most subjects, and all grade levels, as well as college courses—including foreign exchange students, adults learning English as their second language, and students unable to attend school due to illness, surgeries, emotional problems, or pregnancies. Teaching via private instruction became very satisfying. I decided that I had found my niche.

Moving around the country with my military husband during his assignments, I taught in Alaska, Washington, and Montana, finally settling in New York. Years later I returned to my native Ohio to help care for my aging parent. Some of my experience was gained while teaching in a traditional classroom; most was not. Recently, I also began teaching via the Internet.

I have coordinated lesson plans for parents who home-school their children, and I have conducted the instruction for a tutorial program offered by the UAW at the Ford plant in Avon Lake, Ohio, for workers' children. I've prepared students for various examinations, including SAT (Scholastic Aptitude Test), PSAT (Preliminary version of the SAT), ACT (American College Test), GRE (Graduate Record Exam), GED (General Educational Development), OGT (Ohio Graduation Test), OAA (Ohio Achievement Assessment), TOEFL (Test of English as a Foreign Language), PRAXIS (practical application of learning), Catholic High School Entrance Exam, the New York State Regents Exam, the Pipe Fitter's Licensing Exam, and Broker's Licensing Exam.

I teach skills in organization, study, time management, and efficiency while I am teaching the subject material; and—importantly—I encourage my students to become independent from me.

I have been the guest speaker at various PTA/PTO meetings. In 2007, I was inducted into Who's Who Among America's Teachers. In 2012, I published *Teach Your Child to Learn, A Parent's Guide: Simple and Tested Techniques That Work.*

After more than four decades of teaching a variety of subjects to hundreds of students, I still find that one-on-one is stimulating and productive, for both the student and for me—in my case, even well past my formative years.

I love what I do!

Jan Sixt

Chapter Details

What Others Say

Jan Sixt is a gifted educator. She communicates her proven recipes for successful learning to students and parents effectively, methodically, and simply. In her latest book, <u>Teach Your Preschooler to Learn, A Parent's Guide: Preparing Your Toddler for School</u>, Jan offers parents creative and engaging ways to introduce skills from manners to math. Children are our greatest investment. Buying a copy of this book for a new parent or for oneself is the wisest gift you could ever hope to give or receive. Your child's future will definitely be your most profound investment.

——**Deena LaVigne, Usui Reiki Master, Certified Reflexologist, Avon Lake, Ohio.**

I would be remiss if I didn't state that Jan and I met at a Field Day at elementary school for our older children about 30 years ago, and quickly became friends. My high regard for her tutoring ability results from her periodically helping my children, and the children of friends, master a troublesome concept or educational skill. That they respected her, and willingly sought her help, further illustrates that she can clarify and transmit ideas and thoughts in an easily intelligible manner. How pleased I will be to share these books (<u>Teach Your Preschooler to Learn and Teach Your Child to Learn</u>) with those I know who have preschool and school-aged children.

—**Janet Benjamins, Tutor at Erie Community College, Orchard Park, NY; former instructor at Villa Maria College, Buffalo, NY and Northeastern University, Boston, MA.**

Index

www.ingramcontent.com/pod-product-compliance
Lightning Source LLC
LaVergne TN
LVHW051154080426
835508LV00021B/2619